Loss of a Child

Donald Anthony Hines

DEDICATION

This Book is dedicated to my son Aiden Michael Hines (October 20, 2009 – August 13, 2010). Aiden daddy misses you and not a day goes by that I do not think about you! This is a short book as I just give a brief look at the situation. It was too hard to do otherwise.

CONTENTS

Acknowledgments   i

1   Birth   1

2   We have a Son   4

3   Finally Home   5

4   The Results   9

5   Loss   12

ACKNOWLEDGMENTS

I would like to thank my family and all the doctors involved. This was and still is a hard tragedy for me and without everyone's support it would be impossible.

1 BIRTH

It was October 19, 2009 and my wife was having contractions. We went to the hospital and they told us that they were false contractions and that everything was fine. Something about it did not seem right to me. My gut was telling me it was not right but, the hospital insisted and released my wife. We were on our way home and I decided to go to another hospital, the doctor there said that the baby seemed to be in destress and recommend that they transfer my wife to the University Medical Center which was the first hospital we were just at. During this conversation, the chief doctor at the University Medical Center called me and said asked me to bring my wife back as soon as possible and that she should not have been released. I explained that we were at another hospital and he said he would arrange for her immediate transfer. After we arrived at the University Medical Center the Chief Doctor explained that the resident doctor we had seen did not consult him before she was released and he apologized to us. He stated that he felt that my wife needed an emergency C-section. By this time, it was early in the morning on October 20, 2009 and I found myself standing in the Operating Room holding my wife's hand while they were performing a C-section. I was lost, I had this deep sick feeling in my stomach from being scared about not knowing what was going to happen. The next thing I remember was standing there by one of the doctors in the Operating Room holding my son in my arms. That sick feeling now gone and feelings of joy and happiness now filled their place. I was so overwhelmed with joy that I could hardly speak when I went out to tell the family. I could barely say anything to our family, I was in tears of joy. I remember I was crying so hard that my father came up to me and asked if I was ok, everyone was asking if everything was ok. Through tears I managed to say "I'm a daddy, we had a boy!" That was the happiest day of my   life.

2 WE HAVE A SON

We had a boy! I was overjoyed and could hardly believe that I was now a father. We named him Aiden, he was a beautiful baby boy. The fear we had from the emergency c- section had now turned to joy. We were told that our son would need to stay in the NICU until he could suck on his own, as he was born premature. Aiden was in the NICU for over 2 weeks and I never left his side. I stayed by his beside 24/7, I told everyone that I was not leaving that hospital without   my   son.

3 FINALLY HOME

We were finally able to bring our son home, everything was going great. A week after we brought Aiden home we had his first doctor's appointment. The doctor told us that when Aiden was in the NICU they found out that he had a genetic disorder. The doctor said the genetic disorder was called NARP and that we needed to see a specialist for this. The doctor said that this disorder was rare and that they were bringing in a specialist on this condition. After several weeks of waiting we were finally able to see the specialist. We had millions of questions. What is NARP? This is what we were told. Neuropathy, ataxia, and retinitis pigmentosa (NARP) is a condition that causes a variety of signs and symptoms chiefly affecting the nervous system. Beginning in childhood or early adulthood, most people with NARP experience numbness, tingling, or pain in the arms and legs (sensory neuropathy); muscle weakness; and problems with balance and coordination (ataxia). Many affected individuals also have vision loss caused by changes in the light-sensitive tissue that lines the back of the eye (the retina). In some cases, the vision loss results from a condition called retinitis pigmentosa.

This eye disease causes the light-sensing cells of the retina gradually to deteriorate.

Learning disabilities and developmental delays are often seen in children with NARP, and older individuals with this condition may experience a loss of intellectual function (dementia). Other features of NARP include seizures, hearing loss, and abnormalities of the electrical signals that control the heartbeat (cardiac conduction defects). These signs and symptoms vary among affected individuals. We were terrified, we didn't know what was going to happen. The doctor told us that it would depend on the percentage of the disorder our son had on how it would affect him. They took blood samples and sent them off to a lab out of state to be tested and we were told that they would call when the results came in.

4 THE RESULTS

It was almost a month later and they finally called and said the results were in and that the doctor wanted to see us. The next day we were at the doctor's office for the results. The doctor came in and told us that the results were not good, our son had a high percentage of the disorder. He said Aiden was 87 percent affected with the disorder. So, what did that mean? We were told that Aiden could have anywhere from minor symptoms to being mentally disabled or worse. The doctor said that it was hard to say with this condition. Our happy world was now turned upside down. Our son's future was uncertain. The doctor put our son on numerous medications for his condition. We were having weekly appointments with the doctor so, they could monitor our son. Aiden was in and out of the hospital numerous times and we were beginning to become a regular fixture at the Children's Hospital. Test after test, appointment after appointment we were at the hospital more than at home.

5 LOSS

It had been months and our son was deteriorating before our eyes. Aiden was now on Home Health and had a nurse coming out several times a week to check on him. He was on a feeding tube and oxygen, nothing was going right. This continued for months. Then in August, 9 months after our son was born We had to take him to the Children's Hospital ER. He was having seizure after seizure, nothing seemed to stop them. Our son was placed in the ICU and was there for almost a week. The doctors asked to talk with us in a conference room, they told us that Aiden was not getting any better and that the only thing keeping him alive was the life support. They told us that we needed to make a decision. How do you make a decision like that, I was beside myself. This is my son, he has his whole life ahead of him. Finally, we knew what was best. Aiden was only suffering like he was. On August 13, 2010 while I was holding Aiden in my arms the doctors turned off his life support, he took his last breath and passed away with me holding him. I don't know how to express how I was feeling. It is not something that I would wish on my worst enemy. Losing your child is difficult, your whole world is torn apart. There are no words that could express my feelings, then or now. A year later the day my son passed away my wife and I had a daughter. She was born on August 13, 2022, exactly a year to the day our son passed away. That day has become one of sorrow and of joy. It has been 6 years since my son passed away and I am still sad and cry on his birthday and on my daughter's birthday.

ABOUT THE AUTHOR

Donald was born in 1982 in Arkansas; He currently lives in China and works as a High School Teacher there. He has multiply college degrees: Associate Degree in Culinary Arts, Bachelor Degree in Criminal Justice and Master Degree in Asian Studies. He has 1 living child named Brianna. He is a Freelance Photographer and an avid wildlife conservation supporter.